NEW DIRECTIONS FOR PHILANTHROPIC FUNDRAISING

Cathlene Williams
Association of Fundraising Professionals

Lilya Wagner
The Center on Philanthropy at Indiana University
EDITORS

ENGAGING YOUTH
IN PHILANTHROPY

Bill Stanczykiewicz
Indiana Youth Institute

EDITOR

NUMBER 38, WINTER 2002

Editor's Notes

THE ANNUAL HOLIDAY party at Shepherd Community Center's preschool and kindergarten at first seemed like nothing more than traditional philanthropy in action. . ., until a compassionate six-year-old taught all a lesson about the true spirit of giving to others.

Countless individuals, primarily through suburban churches and area businesses, had donated toys, clothing, and food to be distributed to children and their families in this impoverished, crime-ridden inner-city community located on the near-east side of Indianapolis. After a morning of academic instruction, games, and lunch, the children would receive these gifts, which are a staple of Christmas season charity.

This year, there would be a new activity: each child received three toys but then was asked to donate one of those toys to an overseas missions project serving poor children in a distant land. The preschoolers and kindergartners made their donations, still glad to have two new toys for themselves, while their parents were grateful for receiving much-needed clothing and food.

One child was absent that day. Brian was in his second year of kindergarten, held back after failing to master the most basic of skills and information during the previous school year. Yes, some children are so challenged—in Brian's case, by living with a drug-addicted single parent in a home with domestic abuse, poverty, and hopeless isolation—that they cannot even pass kindergarten. Another round of family turmoil had prevented Brian from attending the class Christmas party.

When he returned to school, Brian's teacher explained to him what he had missed. She described the toys, the clothing, and the

NEW DIRECTIONS FOR PHILANTHROPIC FUNDRAISING, NO. 38, WINTER 2002 © WILEY PERIODICALS, INC.

food, and she told him how each of his classmates had donated one of their toys to help poor children overseas.

That is when Brian taught us an unforgettable lesson about philanthropy. Before his teacher could give Brian his three toys and the clothing and food that had been reserved for his family—and before he knew that he still would be receiving those gifts despite missing the holiday party—Brian went to his desk. Lifting the desktop, he reached in and pulled out two beat-up little toy cars, the only toys he owned. He played with them every day during recess, but now he decided they would have even more value with someone else. Brian gave those two little toy cars to his teacher, telling her that he wanted to help those poor children in a foreign land—children he had not met, children he could not deny. Neither poverty nor domestic abuse nor a failing school record would prevent Brian from giving to others out of his personal wealth.[1]

Brian's story reminds us that philanthropy is a habit that can be demonstrated, taught, and inculcated at a very young age. When caring adults are intentional about teaching children about giving to others, the children receive lessons that last a lifetime. This simple fact recently was confirmed by a national study conducted by INDEPENDENT SECTOR and Youth Service America. The report reveals that adults who begin volunteering in their youth are twice as likely to volunteer as adults who were not child volunteers. Importantly, adults who were engaged in philanthropic activities as youngsters also are more generous in their financial giving than adults who did not volunteer or donate money during their youth.[2]

Nonprofit managers and professional fundraisers ignore these findings at their own peril. Nothing less than the sustainability of the third sector is at stake. Working with today's youth is the first step in raising tomorrow's dollars.

Thus, the Indiana University Center on Philanthropy was most prescient in selecting the topic of youth philanthropy for the center's annual national symposium held in August 2002. The event, entitled "Taking Fundraising Seriously: Youth and Philanthropy," opened with a thoughtful and inspiring address from Ken Gladish, president and CEO of the YMCA of the USA. Gladish drew on his depth of experience in the nonprofit sector to describe how youth philanthropy is consistent with America's historical traditions of giving and serving.

In Chapter One, Karin Tice opens this edition of *New Directions for Philanthropic Fundraising* with an informative primer on youth and philanthropy. She describes how young people have learned philanthropic behaviors from several sectors within civil society, including community foundations, nonprofit organizations, schools, and government. Importantly, Tice describes outcomes and implications for nonprofit leaders, youth, and society at large.

Extensive research has demonstrated that philanthropic behaviors often are consistent with socioeconomic status. In short, the more income and education a person has, the more likely that person will be to volunteer and make financial donations to charity. But as the opening anecdote about Brian and Shepherd Community Center demonstrates, demographics need not be destiny. Even more convincing is the thorough evidence revealed in Chapter Two by Mary Kirlin, who reports on remarkable results from a YMCA program encouraging civic activity among children and youth. Interestingly, low-income youngsters with lower levels of academic achievement increased their levels of philanthropic activity after completing this program.

The same is true of financially challenged college undergraduates who earned college scholarships that require recipients to participate in community service. These students are the focus of Chapter Three. Cheryl Keen and James Keen explain how these postsecondary students increased their philanthropic values in addition to other personal skills that benefit civic engagement and service to others.

Increased philanthropic activity by young people, especially those younger than age eighteen, can raise significant legal issues. For example, what legal liability do teens and nonprofits face when the adolescents raise money for the organization? Also, can youth serve on boards, and if they do, can they cast deciding votes on board matters? Questions such as these are ably answered in Chapter Four by Paula Allen, a veteran leader in the youth work field.

Allen also demonstrates that these legal issues should not be a barrier to the numerous opportunities inherent in encouraging youth philanthropic activities.

Chapter Five is by Jack Calhoun, whose national leadership and extensive experience provide him with a unique perspective on what is best for children. His conclusion inspires all of us to become actively engaged in the lives of children and youth—in our families and in our communities—not just to develop healthy habits of philanthropy, but for their overall healthy development.

This issue concludes fittingly with a brief essay by teenager Kathryn Kendall, whose philanthropic contributions have provided her with leadership opportunities at the local, state, and national levels. The passionate voice of this high school senior is an inspiration to all in the nonprofit sector who seek to cultivate future generations of philanthropists.

Bill Stanczykiewicz
Editor

Notes

1. This story was related to me by Rev. Jay Height, Shepherd Community Center, in December 2002.

2. "Engaging Youth in Lifelong Service," by Chris Toppe, Sylvia Golombek, and Arthur D. Kirsch. 2002. (www.independentsector.org/programs/research/engagingyouth.html)

BILL STANCZYKIEWICZ *is president and CEO of the Indiana Youth Institute. He previously served as a legislative staff member in the U.S. Senate and as policy director for Community Renewal in the Office of the Mayor in the city of Indianapolis.*

A brief history and overview of youth involvement in philanthropy is followed by a description of a range of models for involving young people. These models can be implemented by community foundations, schools, nonprofits, and governmental organizations.

1

Engaging youth in philanthropy

Karin E. Tice

YOUTH PHILANTHROPY IS part of a wider paradigm shift from viewing youth as problems to be solved to an asset-based approach where youth are seen as resources to engage in community development. Until recently, policymakers, funders, and program planners have focused on youth deficits while developing programs and policies focused on the prevention of particular problems, such as substance abuse, teen pregnancy, and dropout rates. This is changing as youth are recognized as resources and social actors who are able to contribute to their own development, to that of their communities, and to civil society in general. National, regional, and local organizations have been developed to support youth engagement in community development.

This chapter focuses on youth philanthropy—engaging youth in grant making and fund development. In the mid-1980s, only a few isolated youth philanthropy programs existed. Over a decade later, youth involvement in philanthropy has spread to thirty states, in addition to Canada, the Czech Republic, Great Britain, New

NEW DIRECTIONS FOR PHILANTHROPIC FUNDRAISING, NO. 38, WINTER 2002 © WILEY PERIODICALS, INC.

volunteerism, and the nonprofit sector by weaving information and concepts into existing curricula. More than five hundred teacher-developed and tested lesson plans have been created and are free to download from the Learning to Give Web site (www.learningto-give.org). Six hundred teachers in more than thirty states are now using these resources.

In New York City, Common Cents offers youth a chance to raise and distribute money to nonprofits and other worthy causes within their neighborhoods and schools. In 2000, students from over six hundred schools raised $450,000 by gathering pennies. Ameri-Corps volunteers orient school staff to the program and provide support to the schools.

Government

Some city governments are establishing youth councils to guide the spending of funds allocated for youth programs. Others are involving youth in additional roles within government. For example, Youth Commissioners in Indiana are appointed by the governor to serve as a resource to youth in their senate district. Youth Commissioners are involved in fundraising, service, and legislative advocacy.

Support services

Some organizations are specializing in developing important training opportunities as well as written and other resource materials designed to teach young people about the field of philanthropy. Community Partnerships with Youth (www.cpyinc.org) is one organization that serves this role.

Outcomes

Youth philanthropy creates synergies between the fields of philanthropy and youth development. Although significant and important research has been done in each of the two fields, not many studies have focused on youth philanthropy. This is not surprising; most of the youth philanthropy initiatives are relatively new. Many of these initiatives are conducting formative evaluations to develop and strengthen their own work. Most of these evaluation reports are internal documents, and the findings have not been disseminated publicly. Three important documents, by Cretsinger (1999), Youth Leadership Institute (2001), and Garza and Stevens (2002), provide a national view of youth philanthropy in the United States.

This section presents an initial framework for thinking about outcomes related to youth philanthropy and presents some of the key findings from over ten years of evaluation research (1991–2002) focused on the Michigan Community Foundations' Youth Project (MCFYP; www.mcfyp.org). Although much of the research in the field of youth development and civic engagement focuses on important attitudinal changes for individuals, the framework offered here requires a wider-angle lens and a broader methodological tool kit that allows us to capture organizational, community, regional, and policy outcomes. This framework is offered as a starting point to be built on and added to by other initiatives and researchers. There is still much to learn about youth philanthropy within programs and across initiatives.

Documenting outcomes has become increasingly important to funders and nonprofits alike. Questions are being raised about the effectiveness of both funders' and program implementers' efforts. For example, how effective are foundations' strategies? How and to what extent have programs made a difference—for whom and under what conditions? How can we best disseminate what we have learned about effective practices? Increasingly, evaluators are being brought to the table as partners to help answer these questions. A new emphasis on building learning communities is developing.

Since 1989, Michigan YACs have received over $8 million in grants. Over eight thousand young people have participated, and many more young lives have been touched through YAC grant making. MCFYP has created systemic, community-based change, with profound changes in the way youth are engaged in the field of philanthropy, in nonprofits, and in the social fabric of community life. Although not every community has experienced these changes to the same degree, seeds have been planted in every Michigan

They often take their new attitudes, awareness, and ideas about how to involve youth into their other work.

Organizations

When organizations host youth philanthropy programs, the process can change the way they do business. This has certainly been the case for community foundations (Orosz, Tice, and Van Eck, 2002). Requiring grantees to involve youth in proposal development and program implementation can also have spin-off effects for those organizations (Tice, 2003). For example, one youth-serving organization had never asked youth for their input on programming. Now, after receiving several grants from their local YAC, they always include youth in the process. Their positive experience working with young people on the grants made them realize that they had a valuable underused resource available to them.

Communities and neighborhoods

YACs are modeling how to effectively involve youth in an organization and in a community. They are often highly visible within their communities. When YACs are active grant makers and leaders in their geographical service areas—neighborhoods, communities, or even counties—the way people think about involving youth in civic life can begin to change (Tice, 2003).

Regions

MCFYP is a statewide initiative, with statewide and regional-level leadership training opportunities. These purposefully structured opportunities allowed urban, suburban, and rural youth to get to know each other and each other's communities.

One of the strengths of a regional initiative that provides opportunities for joint leadership training is that youth develop personal and working relationships with other youth and adults different from themselves. There are few venues for youth from diverse backgrounds to work together on issues of common concern. Typically, youth are provided opportunities to compete against other youth in academics and sports. YACs provide an opportunity for them to learn how to collaborate.

Youth philanthropy can be a vehicle for national-level funders that want to make a regional impact in a particular area and value the benefits of grant making done at the local level. In Michigan, YAC members have had many opportunities to serve as intermediaries and in local leadership roles for the distribution of statewide grants from national funders. These grants focus on topics that directly affect young people, such as violence prevention, civil rights, smoking prevention, and volunteerism.

For example, Michigan tobacco settlement monies are being routed to local communities through community foundations to fund health-related programs for youth and seniors. One of the stipulations for receiving these dollars is that two YAC members serve on the advisory committees that review proposals and make grant recommendations. Many of these committees have members who are professionals from health-related organizations or programs, such as hospital administrators and nonprofit staff. Often, the young people are the only ones present with any grant-making experience, a role that puts them in a unique leadership position.

Policies can be changed to allow fuller participation of youth in leadership roles. For example, MCFYP youth advisory committee members were active in developing and encouraging the passage of a bill in 1998 that allows sixteen- and seventeen-year-olds to serve as voting members on nonprofit boards.

Regions will benefit as youth who know about and have participated in grant making and fund development move into young adulthood. Findings from a longitudinal study of MCFYP YAC alumni extending from 1993 to the present indicate that youth continue to give and volunteer long after they complete their YAC experiences (Tice, 1998, 2003). For example, in 2002, 93 percent of the youth surveyed ($n = 94$) had given money to charity over the past year, and about half had given amounts over $200. Seventy-three percent of the respondents had volunteered their time during the past year. Of those who said they had volunteered, most indicated they had given between two and ten hours of their time over the past month. Several respondents commented that they were in school and did not have time to volunteer but planned to in the future.

Some youth are pursuing career paths in the nonprofit sector or in the field of philanthropy as a result of their experiences serving as YAC members. Others responded that serving on a YAC had affected their choice of studies or career path. Others are finding ways to stay active as grant makers, leaders, and fund developers through volunteer activities. Of the ninety-four youth responding to the longitudinal survey in 2002, nineteen were serving on non-profit boards, fourteen of those as voting members. Fourteen were serving on community task forces, and seven volunteered as resources for a youth philanthropy initiative. Foundations and non-profits are starting to draw on the pool of these youth leaders who are already knowledgeable about their work for internships, employment, board members, and volunteers.

Key issues

Four key issues have implications for conceptualizing, funding, and implementing youth philanthropy initiatives: involving a diverse group of youth, changing attitudes, developing effective practices, and sustainability.

Involving a diverse group of youth

Youth initiatives are reaching out to include a diverse group of young people, but many comprise white, high-achieving, already actively involved middle-class youth (Youth Leadership Institute, 2001). Findings from the MCFYP evaluation indicate, however, that high-achieving youth who are known leaders and are already involved in many after-school activities are not the most effective YAC members unless they limit their other commitments. Another finding is that the experience of serving on a YAC had more pro-found impacts on young people who were not known leaders. Most important, the most effective creative grant making occurred in YACs with a diverse group of members. With good facilitation, having diverse perspectives at the table forced young people to examine their own stereotypes and to think creatively.

Diversity does not just happen in youth philanthropy; it is achieved intentionally. Active and thoughtful recruitment is necessary to ensure that youth philanthropy initiatives reach diverse groups (ethnic and racial, socioeconomic, and geographical) of young people. Some neighborhoods, school districts, and communities are wonderfully diverse. Others are homogeneous by nature and sometimes even by design. Crossing inner-city urban-suburban or urban-rural lines can enrich participants' experiences but can also challenge organizational and logistical strategies.

Changing attitudes

Effective youth philanthropy often requires both adults and youths to change their attitudes. Adults must learn to let go and allow young people to lead. Depending on their personal and professional backgrounds, this can be difficult. Similarly, young people have to take on a leadership role. YAC members explained that they were used to being told what to do at school and at home. Most had never had an experience where they had significant responsibility. One implication of this finding is that unless adults have had previous experience, youth leadership and empowerment programs will need to offer technical assistance for the adults as well as the young. Youth leadership training opportunities are vital to developing successful youth philanthropy programs.

Developing effective practices

As the field of youth philanthropy becomes more established, one important task is to develop effective practices. Because of the diversity of initiatives, multiple sets of effective practices may exist and indeed may be needed. It will be important to understand for whom the practices are effective and why. For example, what might be an effective practice in a school setting may not work in a community foundation. The Coalition of Community Foundations for

Youth (www.ccfy.org) has taken a leadership role in developing a broader set of principles and best practices for youth and philanthropy (Garza and Stevens, 2002):

- Build structure and capacity.
- Create organizational structures to support a youth philanthropy program.
- Build a youth-friendly environment.
- Develop a grant-making program that builds on community assets to make lasting change.
- Develop youth-adult partnerships.
- Engage youth as decision makers.
- Connect adults as partners.
- Create connections.
- Involve youth from different cultures and backgrounds.
- Expand and promote leadership roles for youth in the community.
- Develop partnerships with community organizations.
- Develop skills and knowledge.
- Provide program training and ongoing support.
- Plan for sustainability.
- Develop sufficient and sustainable sources of funding.
- Involve youth in fund development.
- Assess program activities and outcomes on a regular basis.
- Communicate program accomplishments.

The MCFYP has developed a set of best practices for involving youth in community foundation grant making and fund development. As youth become increasingly involved in the field of philanthropy, they can share their understanding of what is effective, for whom, and under what circumstances and in the process deepen understanding and practice.

Sustainability
Creating endowed youth funds to be advised by youth is one way to ensure that youth grant making persists. Integrating knowledge

about philanthropy and volunteerism into existing curriculum is another way. Policy changes that allow young people to be voting members on nonprofit boards is yet a third. Finally, developing opportunities within foundations, such as internships and opportunities to serve on the board, for young people interested in pursuing careers in philanthropy will help to ensure the sustainability of this idea.

Conclusion

Youth philanthropy is being implemented in many different ways and in a diverse group of organizations. Youth grant makers are engaged as social actors in their communities. They have economic power to leverage and the ability to serve in leadership roles. Building a learning community of youth, program staff, funders, evaluators, and academic researchers is an important next step. Open dialogue and sharing of information and resources can strengthen everyone's efforts.

With the huge generational transfer of wealth on the horizon, there is an unprecedented opportunity to reweave our social fabric. An important challenge for the future is to link elders and young people through meaningful philanthropic and volunteer activity. Youth grant makers and fund developers are important keys to unleashing resources for the common good. On the changing landscape of philanthropy, youth have an opportunity to shape the field and make a significant difference.

References

Cretsinger, M. *Youth Philanthropy: A Framework of Best Practice*. Battle Creek, Mich.: W. K. Kellogg Foundation, 1999.

Garza, P., and Stevens, P. *Best Practices in Youth Philanthropy*. Basehor, Kans.: Coalition of Community Foundations for Youth, 2002.

Orosz, J. J., Tice, E. K., and Van Eck, S. "Crossing the Generational Divide: Community Foundations' Engaging Youth in Grantmaking, Volunteerism and Leadership." In D. Wertlieb, F. Jacobs, and R. M. Lerner (eds.), *Handbook of Applied Developmental Science: Promoting Positive Child, Adolescent, and*

Family Development—A Handbook of Program and Policy Innovations. Thousand Oaks, Calif.: Sage, 2002.

Tice, K. E. *Empowering Youth: Lessons Learned from the Michigan Community Foundation's Youth Project, 1991–1997.* Grand Haven: Council of Michigan Foundations, 1998.

Tice, K. E. *Youth Grantmakers Contribute to Community Foundation Growth.* Grand Haven: Council of Michigan Foundations, 2001.

Tice, K. E. *Youth Grantmakers with Community Foundations: More Than a Decade of Outcomes and Lessons Learned.* Grand Haven: Council of Michigan Foundations, 2003.

Youth Leadership Institute. *Changing the Face of Giving: An Assessment of Youth Philanthropy.* San Francisco: James Irvine Foundation, 2001.

KARIN E. TICE *is a partner at Formative Evaluation Research Associates (FERA), a firm that strengthens nonprofit organizations. She has evaluated youth development initiatives for more than twenty years, and her research on youth and philanthropy has been disseminated internationally.*

This chapter examines what we know about the predictors of civic engagement, the required elements for adults to be civically engaged, and the role that adolescent extracurricular activities play in creating civically engaged adults.

2

Understanding how organizations affect the civic engagement of adolescent participants

Mary K. Kirlin

ORGANIZATIONS AND associations have long been thought to play a critical role in fostering American democracy. As declines in civic engagement are being more widely reported (Putnam, 1995, 2000), nonprofit organizations have increasingly argued that they are key to enhancing civic engagement.

This chapter helps clarify what we know about the predictors of civic engagement, the required elements for adults to be civically engaged, and the role that adolescent extracurricular activities (and, by default, thousands of nonprofit organizations) play in creating civically engaged adults. Studies of current and former participants in a YMCA teen program illustrate the role that non-profit organizations can play in creating civically engaged adults. This research is especially useful for those funding and managing

Note: I thank Michael Leuthner for his research assistance. The research reported here was funded with a grant from the Indiana University Center for Philanthropy.

Finally, despite the concentration of adolescents from higher socioeconomic status (SES) families in extracurricular organizations, adolescents from lower SES families who choose to participate in extracurricular activities participate in adult civic and political activities at rates similar to their higher SES counterparts (Kirlin, 2001; Verba, Schlozman, and Brady, 1995).

Participation in organizations, especially during adolescence, is a key predictor of later civic engagement. The question is why this occurs and how organizations can more effectively encourage civic behaviors in their participants.

Elements necessary for civic engagement during adulthood

Based on surveys of fifteen thousand adults, Verba, Schlozman, and Brady (1995) argue that adult participation in civic life requires three participatory factors: desire to get involved (motivation), the ability to contribute something to the effort (time or money and the civic skills to make the contribution), and some connection to the groups of individuals who ask others to become involved (networks). The authors identify three preadult experiences that affect later civic participation: education, discussion of politics at home, and participation in an extracurricular organization as an adolescent. Organizational involvement is important for adults as well, with religious attendance and organization membership being relevant to political participation. Table 3.1 summarizes the framework that Verba, Schlozman, and Brady (1995) developed identifying activities and experiences that are correlated with adult civic engagement.

Table 3.1 highlights the impact of organizations during adolescence and adulthood. Any of the three elements necessary for adult engagement—motivation, networks, and skills and resources— could be developed by organizational participation, but for adolescents, the activities seem to serve primarily as a mechanism for

Table 3.1. Stages and factors relevant to political participation

Stage/Factor	Brief Description	Comments
Initial Characteristics		
Parents' education	Educational attainment of both parents	Education is highly correlated with civic participation Parental education benefits are passed on to a child before the child's own education benefits take hold.
Gender		Females are slightly less likely to participate than males.
Race or ethnicity		Whites are more likely to participate than other races and ethnicities.
Preadult Experiences		
Exposure to politics at home	Especially discussions of politics while growing up	Exposure generates awareness and political interest.
Individual's education		Education is highly correlated with civic participation.
Extracurricular activities during high school	Clubs and groups other than sports. Sports are negatively associated with civic participation.[a]	These are thought to teach civic skills necessary for later participation and develop interest in politics.
Adult Institutional Involvement		
Job level	Rank in organization, types, and numbers of contacts with others	Higher-level jobs result in more contacts, better skills, and an increased need to understand and participate in public and civic life.
Affiliation with nonpolitical organizations	Clubs, hobbies, special activities	Similar to extracurricular activities, affiliations provide organizations that offer training in civic skills and opportunity to meet community leaders.
Religious attendance	Active member of religious organization	A significant relationship appears to exist between active religious participation and civic engagement, thought to be related to civic skill training and exposure to community issues and leaders.

Source: Verba, Schlozman, and Brady (1995).

[a]This definition has been further refined by others to clarify that involvement in instrumental, but not expressive, organizations is correlated with civic achievement.

developing civic skills. Adult organizational involvement may facilitate both skill development and network connections. Organizations can also encourage attention to public issues; religious organizations have been particularly good at this function. If civic skill development is an important function of adolescent participation in organizations, then Verba, Schlozman, and Brady's three-factor model (1995) has important implications for program design and implementation.

YMCAs in thirty-eight states run Youth & Government (Y&G) programs. The California YMCA, which has been in existence for over fifty years, sponsors a Y&G program, and two surveys of participants in the program provide a base from which to explore these hypotheses.

The YMCA's Youth & Government Program

High school students who participate in Y&G (they are called delegates) have two components of experience in the organization. The first is with their local YMCA; they meet in delegations of ten to fifty students, where activities they participate in include writing legislation to be presented, reviewing cases to be argued, practicing speaking skills, raising money to cover program fees, and creating a cohesive group structure. The second program component involves three statewide conferences where delegates elect officers, take on roles as attorneys and legislators to hear court cases and bills, and attend social activities.

Are Y&G alumni civically engaged?

During the winter of 2000–2001, surveys were sent to 7,900 California Y&G alumni; 806 (10.2 percent) responded to the initial mailing. After a second mailing, there were 1,069 responses (13.5 percent). The survey asked alumni to provide information about their participation in Y&G, other extracurricular activities they undertook during high school, parental employment, a range of current civic attitudes and behaviors, and basic demographics.

Forty-three percent of respondents (467) were eighteen to twenty-five years old, 45 percent (482) were twenty-six to forty years old, and 11 percent (120) were over forty years old. Participants were 72 percent Caucasian, 8.4 percent biracial or multiracial, 8.2 percent Asian–Pacific Islander, 5.7 percent Hispanic, and 2.7 percent African American.

Careful attention was paid to selecting behavioral measures rather than attitudinal measures for the survey, an important but occasionally overlooked distinction. Behaviors reflect engagement and action, whereas attitudes do not always translate into behaviors. (For further information on this point, see Kirlin, 2002b.)

The following self-reported behaviors were measured:

- Voter registration and voting in the 2000 presidential election
- Contacting an elected official or his or her staff by mail, telephone, or in person during the past five years
- Volunteering for a candidate running for national, state, or local office during the past five years
- Attending a meeting of a local board or council such as a school board or town meeting in the past five years
- Working informally with others in the community on some issue or problem in the past five years
- Serving on a board or as an officer in an organization during the past six months

The first four measures reflect actions in the public sector, and the last two can be in any sector. We first tested for overall civic engagement, predicting (based on previous research) that Y&G alumni would have higher levels of civic engagement than the national average. As expected, participation was considerably higher for Y&G alumni than for the general population on all measures of civic engagement and for several subgroups tested, including alumni with less income or education themselves and those whose parents had jobs that did not require a college degree (see Table 3.2). Overall, Y&G alumni participate at much high rates than the national average.

Table 3.2. Measures of civic engagement: California Youth & Government alumni and the general population

Measure of Civic Engagement	General Population	Y&G Alumni	Y&G Alumni from Households Where Neither Parent's Job Requires a High School Diploma	Y&G Alumni with Self or Family Income Below $25,000	Over Age 25 Y&G Alumni with Less Than a Bachelor's Degree
Registered to vote	66%	96%	96%	96%	93%
Voted in last election	54%	87%	89%	84%	82%
Contacted an elected official	34%	48%	41%	22%	37%
Contributed to a campaign	24%	35%	55%	43%	49%
Volunteered for a political campaign	8%	25%	26%	22%	32%
Protested or marched	6%	29%	25%	31%	27%
Attended meeting of local board or council	14%	45%	51%	44%	49%
Worked informally with others on community issue	17%	43%	33%	43%	37%
Member of a board	3%	15%	12%	15%	15%
$n =$		1,069	73	458	76

Sources: For general population: Self-reported registration and reported voting from 1996 election in U.S. Bureau of the Census (2000). All other data are from Verba, Schlozman, and Brady (1995).

The measures fall along a continuum of sorts, with behaviors requiring varying levels of interpersonal interaction (and presumably civic skills). Several of the measures are essentially individual acts, that is, they can be done in isolation and require minimal interaction with others. Individuals who register to vote, vote, and contact an elected official representative are acting largely alone. These types of engagement can also be self-serving, allowing individuals to express their individual preferences rather than participating in the more challenging work of collective decision making. Table 3.2 reveals that these behaviors are most common in both the general population and in the alumni sample.

Working informally with others or being a member of a board falls at the other end of the continuum. Activities at this end require extensive interaction and cooperation with others. Individuals may need to negotiate and compromise to achieve an outcome satisfactory to the decision-making group. This process requires several civic skills: the capacity to articulate a perspective, listen to others, and work to find an acceptable solution. The remaining three measures—volunteering for a political campaign, protesting or marching, and attending a meeting of a local board or council—fall somewhere in between. Clearly, one can stuff envelopes, march, or attend a meeting alone, but some connections are necessary to initiate the activity, and they cannot be done completely privately.

Given previous research, the finding that Y&G alumni are more civically engaged than the general population is not surprising. However, the very high rate of participation in civic activities, especially those that require interaction with others, is promising. Regardless of income and education characteristics of alumni or their parents, Y&G alumni report being significantly more involved than the general population in almost all aspects of civic life. It is in the five measures where some level of interaction with others is required that the differences between the alumni and general population are most striking, supporting the hypothesis that civic skills are being developed during organizational involvement.

There are at least two cautions regarding the data. First, participation in Y&G is voluntary. In most YMCAs, any student who

Table 3.3. Comparing measures of civic engagement between Youth & Government participants and Introduction to Public Affairs students

Measure of Civic Engagement	Strongly Agree			Agree and Strongly Agree		
	Y&G Delegates	Introduction to Public Affairs	z-Score	Y&G Delegates	Introduction to Public Affairs	z-Score
Civic Skill Measures						
I am comfortable expressing my opinions about political issues even if I know that a majority of people will not agree with my position.	53%	13%	5.38*	84%	74%	1.64
I am confident I could contact an elected official regarding an important issue to me.	30%	19%	1.65	63%	53%	1.32
I would be able to explain differing viewpoints on an issue I care about.	49%	10%	5.39*	85%	63%	3.42*
I am aware of what can be done to meet the important needs in my community.	22%	3%	3.56*	73%	47%	3.49*
I would be able to make an effective presentation or speech.	28%	13%	2.37*	74%	66%	1.22
I am aware of the organizations in my community that are involved in issues I care about.	22%	7%	2.67*	65%	43%	2.89*
I have the ability to conduct or plan and run a meeting.	48%	13%	4.83*	83%	66%	2.69*
I would be able to influence a local board or council that deals with community problems, like city-county council or school board.	19%	3%	3.21*	63%	39%	3.17*
I could organize others in my community to address some issue or problem.	16%	3%	2.70*	59%	46%	1.75

Behavior Measures						
It is essential that I participate in the community and public affairs.	24%	13%	1.84	67%	50%	2.22*
I often discuss and think about how larger political and social issues affect my community.	26%	7%	3.15*	72%	43%	3.92*
It is important to volunteer my time for social issues.	30%	13%	2.58*	73%	49%	3.32*
If I were to move to another city, I could register to vote.	59%	27%	4.21*	90%	81%	1.62
I try to find the time or a way to make a positive difference in my community.	20%	7%	2.42*	54%	36%	2.35*
Efficacy Measures						
I feel I have the ability to make a difference in my community.	30%	14%	2.35*	78%	54%	3.28*
I would be able to organize an event to benefit a charity or religious organization.	19%	9%	1.83	69%	67%	0.31
I would be able to organize an annual cleanup program for the local park	21%	4%	3.14*	70%	67%	0.45
I would be able to explain the current public issues to a person who was new to my community.	29%	6%	3.77*	72%	46%	3.55*
I would be able to get the local government to build an addition to the community center.	7%	1%	1.60	31%	16%	2.25*
I would be able to serve on a board or be an officer in an organization.	50%	20%	4.02*	87%	76%	1.94
n =	108	70		108	70	

Note: An asterisk indicates significance at the .05 level.

Preliminary research findings indicate that a four-year, cocurricular service-learning model supports an exemplary group of low-income students in sustaining and deepening their commitments to service. It also provides skills germane to life success as well as unique opportunities for experience and reflection.

3

A developmental study of the Bonner Foundation's scholarship recipients: Impact of a four-year, cocurricular service-learning model

Cheryl Keen, James P. Keen

FOR THE PAST FIVE years, we have been conducting research aimed at yielding a comprehensive portrait of the effect of the Bonner Scholars Program (BSP) on its student participants.[1] Our interest in the BSP stems from our long-term work on clarifying how people develop and sustain commitments to working on behalf of the common good in an age of diversity, ambiguity, and complexity. In 1996, we and our coauthors, Larry Parks Daloz and Sharon Daloz Parks, published *Common Fire: Leading Lives of Commitment in a Complex World*, the culmination of more than a decade of research into this question, largely supported by the Lilly Endowment.

Note: We express our appreciation to the Center for Assessment and Research Alliances at Mars Hill College for comments on the survey drafts and work in receiving completed surveys and preparing the data for analysis.

NEW DIRECTIONS FOR PHILANTHROPIC FUNDRAISING, NO. 38, WINTER 2002 © WILEY PERIODICALS, INC.

two to three hours of meetings, trainings, advising, and coaching. The nonservice hours include intensive retreats, beginning with orientation and ongoing support in areas such as site supervision, mentoring, time management, group and team-building skills, analysis and organizing, leadership development, and structures for ongoing reflection and peer dialogue. In addition, the program provides financial support for up to three "summers of service," each involving at least seven weeks of full-time service.

The program offers scholars $1,050 stipends each semester to support this service and reflection, as well as $5,000 to support two summers of service as well as a $1,600 loan reduction at graduation for students who complete the program. Funds are also available to support community projects. Most students also complete five additional hours of work per week supported by the Federal Work Study Program.

Principal findings of the surveys

Each year, we administer three distinct surveys, designed to gather data at onset, midcourse, and conclusion of participation in the BSP. Responses to the open-ended queries at the end of the surveys suggest that the questions asked on the survey are congruent with the central experiences of the respondents. Although we do not yet have a full longitudinal data set, we can nevertheless make preliminary observations of a tentative nature.

Consistent on the three surveys is a balance of 60 percent female to 40 percent male respondents. A modest skew toward females may result from two campuses' being women's schools, while one campus is all male. Racial balance is consistent across the three surveys, with 66 to 68 percent being Caucasian, 22 to 25 percent African American (about 40 percent of African Americans come from two historically black colleges), 3 to 4 percent Hispanic, 3 to 4 percent Asian American, 0 percent to 2 percent American Indian, and 0 to 2 percent biracial.

The scholars are selected based on merit and financial need. Indeed, they are an exceptional group of students. When compared to incoming freshmen at four-year private colleges across the country, as measured by this year's survey by the Higher Education Research Institute (HERI), in their senior year of high school, incoming Bonner Scholars averaged six hours or more of community service at four times the national rate and were involved in student clubs and activities (a minimum of six hours a week) at three times the national rate. They spent more time studying, engaging in athletics, holding paid jobs, and socializing than was characteristic of incoming freshmen in the HERI survey. Seniors graduated from the BSP reported higher-than-average rates of study when compared to students nationally, an especially impressive profile for busy emerging leaders. In 2001, 85 percent of seniors graduating from the BSP were leaders on their campuses outside the BSP, and this figure has been increasing (75 percent in 1999, 80 percent in 2000). Moreover, 69 percent of first-semester junior BSP participants reported campus leadership roles outside the BSP.

Service had already been a part of the lives of 98 percent of the incoming freshmen. When asked what aspects of their service work are important, very important, or most important for them to develop in the context of the BSP, 97 percent pointed to respecting and embracing diversity, 95 percent to building community on and off campus, 85 percent to furthering faith development while respecting others' practices, 83 percent to working for social justice, 73 percent to developing an international perspective, and 70 percent to maintaining or developing civic engagement. Other studies of service-learning have noted a significant gap between community engagement and civic engagement, so picking up a similar pattern in our data is not surprising. Nevertheless, it is possible to interpret leadership on one's college campus as an authentic form of civic engagement for undergraduates, a point the civic engagement literature often rushes past.[2] Moreover, 71 percent of seniors completing the BSP report that influencing the political structure is important to them, and 60 percent of the juniors and

Conclusion

Our preliminary findings indicate that the four-year, cocurricular service-learning model offered by the BSP supports an exemplary group of financially challenged undergraduates in sustaining and deepening their commitments to service while providing skills germane to life success, as well as opportunities for experience and reflection beyond those that most participants, given the financial pressures of college, would be likely to access during their college years.

The relevance of these findings may extend beyond the BSP model itself to the question of the impact on student learning and development of cocurricular community service more generally. Interestingly, when it comes to research, the interest in curriculum-based service-learning, in which service is tied to particular courses bearing academic credit, now almost totally eclipses interest in the impact of cocurricular service on student development.[4] There are many reasons for this, including the emphasis on curriculum-based service by national organizations such as Campus Compact and the American Association of Higher Education. While we applaud the substantial gains made in the curricular area of practice (we have been involved in these efforts), we believe the BSP impact results point to the priority of a new effort to come to grips with the impact of cocurricular service-learning, particularly because of three reasons:

It has long been and remains a larger enterprise, affecting far more students than curriculum-based service-learning.

It is the area in which students themselves have by far the greatest opportunity for initiating and managing service enterprises. Here it is important to recall that COOL (the Campus Outreach Opportunity League) and other student-based groups played a key role in igniting and generating the emphasis on service that has been spreading through higher education over the past two decades. Cocurricular service continues to have a high profile among undergraduates, if not among researchers.

The role of federal student funding in the form of AmeriCorps Education Awards and new federal work-study guidelines that increase the emphasis on service activities, as well as the trend among colleges and universities to shift at least a percentage of merit-based financial aid to community service expectations, indicates that the great growth area in service-learning over the near term will be in the area of cocurricular rather than in curriculum-based service-learning.

The question of whether learning takes place outside the formal curriculum is an old one. Without rehearsing that debate, we will place ourselves within the long tradition of researchers on higher education of understanding student learning as occurring within the learning environment as a whole, including its sponsored extension beyond the borders of the campus, for example, study-abroad programs and internships (Kolb, 1983; Kuh, 2002; Smith and McCann, 2001). Within this tradition, the formal curriculum is a fundamental aspect of that learning environment but is not tantamount to its whole. From this perspective, the question of what constitutes service-learning can be framed in wider or narrower terms. In the widest terms, service-learning would mean whatever one learns from service. In the narrowest terms (now often employed by researchers), it means what one learns that can be measured against the objectives of a particular course of study. The Bonner Scholars Program, with its emphasis on training, coaching, reflection, teamwork, group dialogue, and student involvement in program and site leadership, stakes out a definition of service-learning that requires the systematic digestion of and generalization from the experience of service—a point of view that looks at service-learning from about middle ground—and a definition that includes most institutionally based cocurricular service as well as most curriculum-based service.

The BSP student impact research can tell us a great deal about a particular model of cocurricular service-learning that is now strongly influential in higher education. But another important role of this research is its vanguard position in the area of service-learning that affects the largest number of students: the area that is cocurricular rather than classroom based. When the research is ready for full publication in the fall of 2003, it will be available to serve as a reference point and as a point of departure for a timely and vigorous new research effort in the area of cocurricular service-learning.

Notes

1. These reports can be found at the Bonner Foundation Web site (www. bonner.org/resources/assessment.htm).
2. Campus Compact's mapping of civic engagement programs has focused on this definition: "those activities which reinvigorate the public purposes and civic mission of higher education" (www.compact.org).
3. A summary of this report is available at http://www.gseis.ucla.edu/ heri/norms_pr_01.html.
4. See, for instance, the roster of papers presented at the Second International Conference on Service-Learning Research, held at Vanderbilt University in the fall of 2002.

References

Daloz, L. P., Keen, C., Keen, J., and Parks, S. D. *Common Fire: Leading Lives of Commitment in a Complex World.* Boston: Beacon Press, 1996.

Kolb, D. *Experiential Learning: Experience as the Source of Learning and Development.* Upper Saddle River, N.J.: Prentice Hall, 1983.

Kuh, G. *From Promise to Progress: How Colleges and Universities Are Using Student Engagement Results to Improve Collegiate Quality.* National Survey of Student Engagement annual report. Bloomington: Indiana University Center for Postsecondary Research and Planning, 2002.

Smith, B. L., and McCann, J. (eds.). *Reinventing Ourselves: Interdisciplinary Education, Collaborative Learning, and Experimentation in Higher Education.* Bolton, Mass.: Anker Books, 2001.

CHERYL KEEN AND JAMES P. KEEN *share a position as college professor at Antioch College and an appointment as senior research fellows at the Bonner Foundation in Princeton, New Jersey.*

Incorporating youth as decision makers in a nonprofit organization presents certain legal questions about their status, particularly if they serve on boards of directors.

4

Youth and philanthropy: Legal issues, practical consequences

Paula Allen

SINCE THE LATE 1980s, great strides have been taken in involving youth in philanthropic activities, with at least two movements at the forefront: youth grant making and service-learning. Today, thousands of young people volunteer through their schools and faith-based and community-based organizations, and hundreds more serve as grant makers through community foundations, United Ways, and programs like Youth as Resources (YAR, whose chapters nationwide encourage youth-led philanthropy and community service projects).

Research undertaken by the INDEPENDENT SECTOR (1998) shows that adults who participated in charitable activities when they were young tend to volunteer and donate to charities at a significantly higher rate than those who did not. From this perspective, youth philanthropic activity should be part of any discussion of adult fundraising, because it makes sense to educate and involve young people with one's particular cause. As they grow and expand their personal financial resources, their knowledge of and past

NEW DIRECTIONS FOR PHILANTHROPIC FUNDRAISING, NO. 38, WINTER 2002 © WILEY PERIODICALS, INC.

participation with community organizations will guide their interests in community problem solving and giving.

"The fundamental change is yet to come," says Steven Culbertson, CEO of Youth Service America. "The experiences young people are gathering now mean that in the future, as they get older, we're likely to see much more progressive and involved people in positions of power" (Blum, 2000, pp. 1–2).

While adults have played a major role in providing opportunities for youth to learn about and participate in volunteer activities, much of the increased interest in philanthropy is coming from youth themselves. Many young people are more knowledgeable about social issues than their parents' generation, in part because information is readily available on the Internet. As schools incorporate service-learning into their curricula, classes help motivate youth to become civically engaged and explore the community on their own. Community service requirements at some schools also boost local volunteerism and help educate students about community resources and needs, with the result that youth continue their volunteer participation after the required service ends. Programs such as YAR, which support group volunteer projects with small grants, offer new ways for youth to make and interact with friends, heightening the appeal of volunteering.

"For the first time in the history of our country, we are looking to kids starting at age 12 and 13 as real philanthropic assets in our communities," says Joel J. Orosz, former program director at the W. K. Kellogg Foundation (Blum, 2000, p. 1). The Kellogg Foundation has been a leader in encouraging youth philanthropy through a matching-grant program to community foundations in Michigan that trains and involves teens in fundraising and grant making.

How are youth best engaged with voluntary organizations to use their skills and experiences, and what are the legal and political consequences of including youth in real positions of influence—on governing boards and planning committees and in fundraising and distribution? What are the consequences for the nonprofit world, as increasing numbers of youth are exposed to philanthropy?

Involving youth in a meaningful way

Major fundraising institutions have begun to realize the advantages associated with involving youth as resources in their organizations. Kendall, Lesko, and Radmer (2002) write,

> Put simply, involving youth as equal partners is a new way of doing business for many United Ways. This philosophy means valuing and respecting young people beyond an intrinsic "future value" but as unique individuals who can make important contributions today. . . .
>
> Young people can be involved in *all aspects* of your United Way's work. Young people can work alongside adults as campaign volunteers or loaned executives. They can serve as full members of vision councils, the campaign cabinet, citizen review teams, allocations panels, policy committees, or even the board of directors [p. 4].

United Way of Central Indiana realized the advantages of youth participation when it merged with YAR in 1993. The National Crime Prevention Council had piloted the YAR model in Indianapolis, Evansville, and Fort Wayne in 1987, and five years later the grant-making program had really taken off. YAR of Central Indiana, which currently involves more than seventy teenagers as grant makers in six counties, awards small grants for volunteer service projects designed and run by local youth groups. Youth project participants, ages eight through eighteen, come from diverse settings in urban, suburban, and rural environments, supported by sponsoring organizations like schools, scout troops, churches, and correctional institutions.

"The presence of youth on our boards reminds adult members of the variety of perspectives that should be considered when making decisions about human care issues," says Ellen Annala, CEO of United Way of Central Indiana. "Their ideas can enhance services and increase the impact United Way can have in central Indiana communities" (Youth to Serve on United Way's County Advisory Boards, 2002, p. 1). Indeed, program evaluations of United Way of Central Indiana have demonstrated that YAR participants increase their awareness and knowledge of local problems

Is it legal?

Incorporating youth as decision makers in a nonprofit organization presents certain legal questions about their status, particularly if they serve on boards of directors. In seven states (Colorado, Florida, Georgia, Nevada, New Jersey, Pennsylvania, and Utah), it is illegal for people under the age of eighteen to serve as voting members on boards of directors. Youth in these states may serve on boards in a nonvoting capacity and may serve and vote on board subcommittees and task forces. New York State law requires board members to be eighteen in most cases, but sixteen-year-olds may serve in certain educational, youth development, or delinquency prevention programs.

Youth in Michigan and Minnesota can serve as voting members of boards of directors with certain restrictions. In Michigan, youth must be sixteen or seventeen years old, providing their number does not exceed more than half of the total directors required for a quorum. In Minnesota, youth of any age may serve on boards, providing the majority of directors are at least eighteen years old.

In the remaining forty states and the District of Columbia, the law is silent on whether young people can legally serve as voting members. In these states, boards with youth members need to exercise care to prevent raising issues of liability, specifically in the area of contract law. It is recommended that youth be required to abstain on votes involving contracts, particularly when the youth vote could influence the outcome of a contract decision.

An investigation into the legal question of whether minors may serve on the boards of nonprofit agencies in Indiana produced uncertain results. Each state agency consulted—including the Office of Senator Richard Lugar, the Department of Education, the Office of the Attorney General, the Office of the Secretary of State, the Professional Standards Board, the State Election Board, and the Indiana University Law School Library—gave an unofficial opinion on this legal question, and there was no uniformity of response. There was general agreement, however, that including youth on nonprofit boards presented risks. Only the Office of the Secretary of State was able, after brief research, to provide a legal opinion.

According to Rebecca Longfellow, former counsel and deputy director of the Corporate Division, Office of the Secretary of State, there are no qualifications for officers of nonprofit agencies except those provided in the organizations' articles of incorporation and bylaws. Unless prohibited by the bylaws, minors may serve on the board of any nonprofit organization.

Even so, Longfellow thinks that youth on boards "make a weak link" in that they cannot legally enter into any contracts until they are eighteen years old.

Thus far, no one has undertaken a more extensive examination of contract law and common law to look at what minors can and cannot do legally, as well as case research to see if anyone has brought suits against boards with underage members. At issue is to what extent youth serving on a board have control of the vote.

Another issue is that some local youth organizations are chartered through national organizations (for example, Boy Scouts). In such cases, an examination of the legal code in the state of origin would also be in order. In the case of Boy Scouts, their charter is through the state of Texas, which is less clear than Indiana regarding the legal status of youth on boards. (Although Texas is silent on youth board membership, state law does require incorporators to be eighteen years old.)

Board members of all ages receive some protection under laws that limit the liability of volunteers who are connected with nonprofit organizations. The measures protect volunteers from liability in cases where they are not personally negligent and prevent them from having to pay damages disproportional to their responsibility.

Even with a clear legal path for youth board membership, organizations must check their bylaws for prohibitions to youth membership. Taking the trouble to change the bylaws to include young people sends a strong message to them that they are respected and valued.

An additional consideration is the issue of parent or guardian consent. Communicating with parents alleviates their concerns about how their young person is spending his or her time and often

- Communication skills. In addition to learning how to sell their ideas, they learn team building, diplomacy, tact, and how to build consensus.
- Confidence and networking skills. They make contacts that can be helpful in the job market as they grow and mature.

There are a few drawbacks to youth participation as well. The teen years are an important developmental stage of life, and many new experiences and activities vie for young people's attention. Youth are relatively inexperienced when addressing legal, political, or policy questions. They may have difficulty articulating their point of view in a mostly adult setting, particularly if a lone youth is serving on a board or committee. There are logistical challenges, such as needing rides to meetings. Some organizations, such as small agencies without directors' and officers' liability insurance coverage, may be concerned with legal liability.

Overcoming obstacles

Researchers at the University of Wisconsin in 2000 found that adults and organizations experienced significant positive change after actively involving youth in decision-making roles. Although this work identifies the need for more research to understand the nature and extent of the impact, experienced practitioners readily point out the benefits (some of which are listed above) and the hurdles they had to overcome to make youth participation in their organizations work. Barriers to success are both perceptual and logistical.

Perceptual barriers

- The perception that youth are lacking in intelligence or ability, and adults' low expectations of their behavior.
- The perception that including youth in decision making means a lot of extra work for staff and board.
- The perception that youth lack the ability to maintain confidentiality regarding board decisions and client information.

- The expectation that a few youth board members speak for their entire age group.
- The perception of youth as lacking the capacity to raise funds on behalf of the organization.
- The unwillingness by adults to give up some power in order to empower youth decision makers.

Logistical barriers

- The inflexibility of agency boards in altering time and setting to accommodate potential youth members.
- The unwillingness of adults to translate the operational language of their agencies for easy understanding by young people.
- Bylaws that impede the inclusion of youth membership and an unwillingness to change them.
- Lack of legal clarity.
- Costs associated with including youth, such as staff time, training, revised materials, transportation, and food.
- Poor recruitment strategy for including youth. Organizations that pursue top student leaders may find them to be overcommitted elsewhere. Recruiting youth perceived as in need of help is well intentioned but not effective. Youth, like adults, need to be recruited and selected because of their talents, abilities, and networks.
- High turnover rate of youth as they move on to higher education and the need to replace them more frequently.

Youth participation survey

To incorporate youth participants in decision making, structures may have to change, as well as attitudes and behaviors that have become entrenched. An informal look at seventeen organizations serving youth in central Indiana provided some insight as to how organizational culture affects success with including young people.

The seventeen youth-serving organizations that I surveyed included twelve that identified themselves as mission focused on agencies have joined the cause. Youth involvement has taken many forms, as volunteers, donors, community problem solvers, and even founders of organizations. Equally noteworthy, studies show that involvement as youth is a significant factor influencing how adult volunteers and donors behave.

There is no uniformity of opinion regarding the legal issues surrounding youth participation as decision makers, fundraisers, and grant makers. State laws differ, with the majority of states opting to remain silent on the issue of age. Even so, those in the field agree that this kind of youth participation presents risks, and organizations need to exercise care to avoid liability issues.

There is growing evidence that youth participation has resulted in significant positive changes for adults and for organizations in the nonprofit sector. (This is in addition to the more obvious benefits that youth gain from their involvement with voluntary organizations and causes.) As volunteers, youth are proving to be valuable assets and resources through their giving of time and talent. They are also an untapped donor pool, whose understanding of community issues and volunteer experiences will significantly influence the giving choices and decisions they will make as adults.

Many excellent resources are available to help nonprofit organizations learn the best ways to incorporate youth into their decision-making environments. What remains is for adults to recognize that youth can be important resources for furthering organizational missions, that youth have the time, energy, and vitality to make a difference in organizational outcomes, and that an investment in youth leadership increases the social capital that makes communities flourish.

Is youth involvement with philanthropic organizations a trend, or is it becoming part of our philanthropic culture? What is the local and collective impact of youth-adult partnerships? What impact does youth participation have on organizations over time? What factors are known to influence success across contexts? How does youth philanthropic activity fit into the larger field of philanthropy? There are many areas in this new field that would benefit from further research and evaluation. Most notably, there is little information available about youth involvement in fundraising.

Recently, a joint effort by researchers at the University of Wisconsin and the Innovation Center for Community and Youth Development identified six areas of potential research related to youth involvement. Its report, *Youth Involvement for Community, Organizational and Youth Development: Directions for Research, Evaluation and Practice* (2002), highlights a series of questions generated by a group of youth and adult researchers and practitioners. In recommending their research agenda, the authors declare that it is essential that young people be involved in both design and implementation.

In a recent issue of the *Chronicle of Philanthropy*, Eisenberg (2002) urges the nonprofit world "to do a better job of seeking out and attracting youth to its causes. . . . They are the pool of talent from which future generations of leaders will have to come. But they need encouragement, applause, and support" (p. 64).

Young people have discovered the power of civic participation, and voluntary organizations are the better for it. Time will tell whether youth participation is a passing trend or a permanent addition to the philanthropic landscape.

References

Blum, D. E. "High-School Senior and Peers Are a Growing Force for Philanthropy." *Chronicle of Philanthropy*, Jan. 13, 2000.

Eisenberg, P. "Philanthropy Must Do More to Recognize the Young Who Do Good." *Chronicle of Philanthropy*, Apr. 18, 2002.

INDEPENDENT SECTOR. "America's Teenage Volunteers: Civic Participation Begins Early in Life." [www.independentsector.org] 1998.

Kendall, A., Lesko, W., and Radmer, M. *Youth as Equal Partners: A United Way Guidebook on Youth Involvement.* Alexandria, Va.: United Way of America, 2002.

Lesko, W. S., and Tsourounis, E. *Youth! The 26 Percent Solution.* Kensington, Md.: Activism 2000 Project, 1998.

Sazama, J., and Young, K. S. *Your Guide to Youth Board Involvement and the Law.* Somerville, Mass.: Youth on Board, 2001.

University of Wisconsin and the Innovation Center for Community and Youth Development. *Youth Involvement for Community, Organizational and Youth Development: Directions for Research, Evaluation and Practice.* 2002.

tough kids, who is still with it: Paula Allen, currently director of Youth as Resources of Central Indiana, which encompasses six counties and YAR boards. The other is the Lilly Endowment's Willis Bright, who walks his words and backs his words with money and commitment, and who said in Evansville as we were putting YAR together, "Jack, we've got to get kids on the board, along with adults giving grants to kid-run programs."

"Youth in philanthropy" can be defined in many ways. A broad definition is of young people giving time and talent to their communities, or young people involved in the formal philanthropic granting process. Matt Rosen, writing for the Youth Leadership Institute, suggests the following definitions (2001, p. 12):

- Young people giving time and talent to their communities
- Helping young people answer the question, "What do I care about?"
- Involving youth in traditional, organized philanthropy
- Spurring and nurturing the idea and ideal of public service

Ken Gladish, executive director of the YMCA of the USA, has defined youth in philanthropy as "an approach to empowering or establishing young people as community leaders."

Youthful testimony

Whatever the framework and whatever the lens, I believe the message of the power of engaging youth is best heard through the voice of a young person.

YAR asks youth to spot issues about which *they* are concerned. Youth design the projects and run them. YAR is not a program by adults for youth, but by youth with adults for the community. YAR took off like a rocket. But would it also work with the kids locked up, the kids in group homes? Would it work with the lonely? the abandoned? the angry?

I got a call eight weeks ago at about 6:30 at night. The voice, heavy and slow, asked, "Do you remember me?" The voice was distinctive. I said, "Keep talking."

"Jack, is it you? Do you remember me?" And his face and his story slowly came back to me: Donnie Hinkle. I recalled that I had spent only about eight hours with Donnie in my life: a couple of hours at the group home and a few hours when they unveiled the playground that the youth in the group had built for the community. And I said, "Donnie, of course, I know you! Why are you calling?"

Donnie said, "Jack, remember when you came to the group home? You said you were going to try YAR with kids who had gotten into trouble, and they could be an example of proving to the community that they were valuable. I just wanted to tell you that Monday, I'm starting as a member of the Indiana Iron Workers Union making twenty-three dollars an hour, working on the expansion of the Indianapolis airport."

He continued, "I just wanted to call to thank you."

I replied, "Donnie, I did very little. You did it."

He said, "You were one of the two that believed in me." (The other was someone he now calls his "grandfather," a person who volunteered to be his mentor when Donnie was in the group home and someone who has stuck with him for a decade.)

Donnie talked about this faith in him: "When I built that playground and all those people congratulated me, I knew I could do good things in my life."

This is an extraordinary story. What a gift: not only to hear back but to affirm the fact that Donnie's story is at the very heart of youth in philanthropy.

It is so very important in this post-9/11 world of fear and suspicion, of corporate greed gone amok, that this particular gospel, this particular light—this belief in youth—that we are all holding high continues to burn brightly.

A 1997 Public Agenda Survey (Farkas, 1997) commissioned by the Advertising Council found that two-thirds of adults did no particularly like youth. "Undisciplined, disrespectful, unfriendly. . . .

We even fear them" were some of the phrases used. A former Texas attorney general, Dan Morales, would say that out of a thousand kids, 997 are OK, good or wonderful, but who drives public policy? Three.

To the extent that public policy is a promise, we do have a very clear promise: "If you screw up and you are bad, we are here waiting for you." Thirty-five thousand dollars a year for jail. But where is the companion promise that says, "We are here to elicit the very best from you and to engage you as partners in the issues of community building"?

I believe deeply that we hold a sacred trust and are entrusted with a difficult mission. Some foundations are trying to infuse this particular message into schools. Among them are the Michigan Foundation's Learning to Give curriculum. Some government agencies are devoting some funding for youth involvement. I believe Oakland, California, has done that, as has San Francisco. But the foundation community serves as the huge engine for the work of youth involvement.

The work of Rob Collier from the Council of Michigan Foundation has been inspiring to so many across the country. He reports that there are about 350 Youth in Philanthropy programs in more than thirty states and eight countries. These young people often leverage other resources, and they can be good fundraisers and tough grant reviewers. In one of YAR's grant sessions that I sat in, a youth board member asked, "Well, do you have a hardware store in your neighborhood?" The petitioner, who was his peer, said, "Yes." He replied, "Get the hardware store to contribute the nails. We're striking them from your budget."

Why youth involvement are strategies critical

Lynn Leonard, of the Ewing Marion Kauffman Foundation, has talked about the impact of youth involvement across the board on kids, on organizations' funders, and on youth themselves. Kimberly Schroeder, of the Dekko Foundation, has talked about pushing the spark of philanthropy down to very young children, as low as third grade.

That is the "what," but we have to pay close attention to the "why." Why are these youth involvement policies of such critical importance?

Most policies regarding youth are based on one of three pillars: controlling kids, that is, punishment and control; fixing and helping kids; and what is probably best described as gritting your teeth and getting through it as a parent or caregiver, that is, just trying to get through the teen years.

Certainly, we need control and punishment, and we need the best in healers, those who would mentor, who would untangle abuse and dyslexia and other ills. But very rarely do we underscore the heart of what we are trying to do.

We must advocate for another policy formulation, one that is embraced by a single word: *claim*. We know that many youth feel disconnected from family, school, and community. But the opposite of disconnection is not repair; it is passionate involvement. So many youth know this, and many of them act out of their loneliness and pain. Said one juvenile murderer to me when I was commissioner of youth services in Massachusetts, "I'd rather be wanted for murder than not wanted at all."

The heart of the problem

Our policy discussions tend to identify all of the teen problems: pregnancy, drug abuse, violence, and others, but discussions often miss the very heart of the problem: the aloneness, the isolation, the disconnection, and the hopelessness. This connection is the core element that makes our society work: those who are involved help the community and, by extension, the republic work.

The gaping hole for many of today's youth is a lack of a sense of place in the community. The absence of bonding strikes at the very heart of what it means to belong, to be a contributing member of society. We can describe youth in philanthropy in political terms as attempting to get youth to be signatories of the social contract or psychologically as bonding—the message that "you are part of us, and we need you."

I passionately believe that our approach to the youth issue that rests solely on the pathological will not work. I also maintain that when we ask something even from the most troubled and troubling of youth, we imply that there is something of worth that these youth have to give. When I ran the pretrial diversion programs in the early 1970s in Massachusetts, I was struck by the number of kids who would say, "Yeah I ripped off that guy, but I had a lousy lawyer." The statement was a curious conjunction of admission of guilt and denial of any human connectedness: "The judge was this or that. It was somebody else's fault." So I had these young people meet their victims, with community people as mediators. The undergirding thesis was dual: you are responsible and—the more powerful and implicit message—you have something of worth to give back. At the time I called it "justice as reconciliation." Today it is called "restorative justice."

Justice as reconciliation is one of YAR's taproots. Something powerful happens to youth when we ask for their help. By asking something in return, we begin a process of building community. Such an approach is critically important for nine reasons:

1. We need talented and capable workers.
2. We have got to learn and relearn that which we always know: experiential learning is critical.
3. Youth service represents part of the dues we all must pay as members of a democratic society.
4. There are critical tasks that need to be done.
5. Young people are told that they are loved, but many, especially those from fragmented or nonexistent families, do not feel they have a place, do not feel they are needed.
6. Youth spend less time with adults than ever before. This approach could bring them into partnership with adults.
7. Such an approach encourages a positive sense of self.